Text by Frederick C. Klein

# For the Love of the Red Sox

## An A-to-Z Primer for Red Sox Fans of All Ages

Illustrations by Mark Anderson

foreword

" In my first few years with the Red Sox, people used to compare me to **Phil Rizzuto** and **Pee Wee Reese**. It wasn't quite on the same level as the arguments about whether **Ted Williams** was better than Joe DiMaggio, or who was the best center fielder, Mickey Mantle, Willie Mays, or Duke Snyder, but there were debates, especially in Boston and New York, over which of us was the best shortstop. Rizzuto and Reese are both in the Hall of Fame, and they both deserve to be there. I'm in the Boston Red Sox Hall of Fame, and that's good enough for me, especially now that they are world champions.

And speaking of the Red Sox Hall of Fame, most of the other players in this unique book are there too. I hope you enjoy reading about them, some of the greatest Red Sox players of all time, accompanied by the wonderful illustrations, which bring the players and their eras to light. "

— **Johnny Pesky**

# "A" is for "Again!"

The Sox fans' cry
When the Rockies were beaten and
The trophy held high.

**The Boston Red Sox went 86 years without a World Series** triumph but broke that streak with a vengeance by winning baseball's biggest prize in 2004 and again in 2007. The 2004 team came back from a three-games-to-none deficit to defeat their archrivals, the New York Yankees, in the American League Championship Series, then swept the St. Louis Cardinals in the Series. The 2007 club followed a similar course, falling behind the Cleveland Indians three-games-to-one in the ALCS before rallying, then thumping the Colorado Rockies in a four-game World Series in which it outscored its foe, 29 runs to 10.

# "B" is for Babe Ruth.

The team sold him, and worse,
Had to live 86 years
With the Bambino's curse.

**George Herman "Babe" Ruth came to the major leagues in 1914 at age 19** as a left-handed pitcher, and in that capacity helped the Red Sox win the World Series in 1915, 1916, and 1918. Short of cash, the team sold him to the New York Yankees for $125,000 in 1920. In New York, where he was moved to the outfield full time because of his batting ability, "the Bambino" rewrote baseball's power-hitting records and led the Yanks to numerous championships. His so-called curse was a sports-page invention, but 1918 remained the Red Sox's last World Series title until 2004.

# "C" is for Clemens,

Whose nickname is "Rocket."
This fastballing Texan
Had fans in his pocket.

**Roger Clemens joined the Red Sox in 1984 out of the University of Texas**, and went on to tie the great Cy Young for the team's all-time pitching record with 192 wins over the next 13 seasons. Big and hard-throwing, the right-hander won the American League best-pitcher awards named for Young in 1986, 1987, and 1991, and led the league in strikeouts three times. His later career with the New York Yankees earned him two World Series rings.

# "D" is for Dice-K,

The man from Japan.
He came to the States
On a championship plan.

**Daisuke ("Dice-K") Matsuzaka didn't come to Boston cheap:** in the winter of 2006 the Sox paid his former team, the Seibu Lions of the Japanese League, $51 million to release him and gave him a six-year contract worth $54 million. He rated it because, at age 26, he'd been the best pitcher in his native land and led his national team to victory in the 2006 World Baseball Classic. The acquisition paid off. Showing a potent variety of pitches, the right-hander posted a 15-12 won-lost record during the 2007 regular season, won the seventh game of the ALCS versus Cleveland, and won Game 3 of the World Series.

# "E" is for Evans,

## A right fielder with class.
## No gardener ever covered more grass.

**Dwight Evans played for the Red Sox from 1972 through 1990**. He ranks second in club history for most games played (2,505) and is among the team's top 10 in just about every career hitting category. He was an eight-time Gold Glove winner at his demanding position. He had great fielding range and base runners rarely challenged his arm.

# "F" is for Fisk,

## Who kept Sox hopes alive
## With his barely fair homer in '75.

Carlton "Pudge" Fisk, born in Bellows Falls, Vermont, started at catcher for the Red Sox from 1972 through 1980, winning All-Star Game berths in seven of those seasons. He is best known for his home run off the left-field foul pole at Fenway Park in the twelfth inning of Game 6 of the 1975 World Series, which gave Boston a 7–6 win over Cincinnati. Fisk set records for durability behind the plate over a 24-season big-league career.

# "G" is for Green Monster,

Fenway's left-field wall.
The hits clanging off it
Ring a loud wake-up call.

**Boston's Fenway Park, opened in 1912, is the major leagues' oldest stadium,** and its close, towering left-field fence, called the "Green Monster," is its outstanding feature. The wall stands an inviting 310 feet from home plate. It turns routine fly balls into hits and changes drives that would be home runs elsewhere into singles or doubles. Originally covered with advertising signs, it was first painted solid green in 1947. Seats were installed atop it for the 2003 season.

# "H" is for Hooper,

A defensive gazelle.
On four pennant winners
He did his job well.

**Harry Hooper joined the Red Sox in 1909 with a college degree**, which was rare for a ballplayer of his era. He quickly became a regular as a leadoff hitter and right fielder. From 1910 through 1915 he teamed with center fielder Tris Speaker and left fielder Duffy Lewis to form what is still regarded as one of baseball's greatest outfields. Hooper was the only man to play on all four of the Red Sox's World Series champion teams (1912, 1915, 1916, and 1918) in the 20th century's second decade.

# "I" is for Intimidating,

Josh Beckett's middle name. When playoff time comes He's on top of his game.

**Beckett is one of baseball's best young pitchers** and someone who saves his best for the biggest games. In 2003, at age 23, the hard-throwing right-hander pitched the underdog Florida Marlins to the World Series title, shutting out the Yankees in the sixth and deciding game. He was even better for the Red Sox in 2007, going 20–7 during the regular campaign and winning all four of his postseason starts. His seven-inning, one-run stint in Boston's 13–1 first-game victory over the Colorado Rockies set the stage for the Sox's World Series sweep.

# "J" is for Jim Rice,

## Who battered the fences with line drives
## That shattered opponents' defenses.

**Over a 16-season Major League career** (1974–1989), all in Boston, Rice hit 382 home runs and batted in 1,451 runs, putting himself third on the team's all-time list in both categories. The muscular outfielder was an eight-time All-Star Game selection. In 1978, when he batted .315, hit 46 homers, and drove in 139 runs, he was voted the American League's Most Valuable Player.

# "K" is for Kinder,

## He gave it a try, but in his best seasons
## The Sox came up shy.

**Ellis Kinder, a right-handed pitcher, didn't reach the major leagues until age 32,** but once he got there he posted 102 victories over 12 seasons. His best year in Boston was 1949, when the Red Sox battled the Yankees down to the season's final day only to fall short by one game. He won 23 games that season and held the Yanks to a single run in seven innings in the head-to-head finale, which the team eventually lost, 5–3. He later excelled as a relief pitcher.

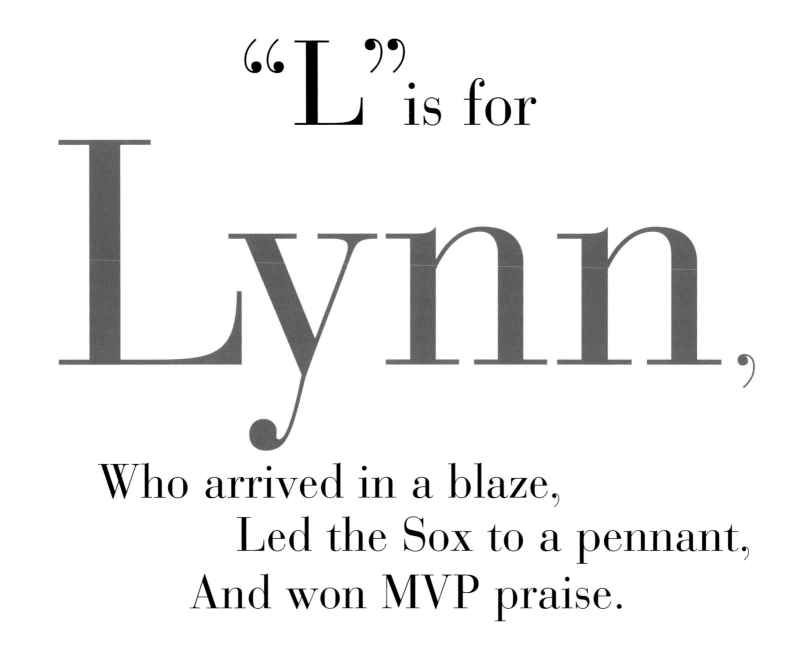

# "L" is for Lynn,

Who arrived in a blaze,
Led the Sox to a pennant,
And won MVP praise.

**Few players have had a debut campaign as good as Freddie Lynn's.** With the pennant-winning Red Sox in 1975, the California native hit .331, drove in 105 runs, and became the first player to capture both Rookie-of-the-Year and Most-Valuable-Player awards in the same season. Lynn, a center fielder, had other fine years—with the California Angels and the Baltimore Orioles as well as with the Red Sox—but none was as good as his first.

# "M" is for Martinez,

Whose arm is a whip.
Few pitchers' deliveries
Have quite as much zip.

**Pedro Martinez, from the Dominican Republic,** has a slender build, but generates enough arm speed to make himself one of the dominant pitchers of the new century. In his seven seasons pitching for the Red Sox (after coming to Boston in a 1997 trade with the Montreal Expos), he won 117 of his 154 decisions and captured the American League's Cy Young Award in 1999 and 2000. His competitive nature and strikeout flair endeared him to Boston fans.

# "N" is for

# Nomar.

That's Garciaparra.
His towering home runs
Can hardly go "fartha."

**Anthony Nomar Garciaparra is a rare good-fielding shortstop** who also has power at the plate. In his seven seasons after joining the Red Sox full time in 1997, he hit 25 or more home runs four times and won American League batting titles in 1999 (.357) and 2000 (.372). Garciaparra—who was traded to the Cubs in the summer of 2004 and now plays for the Los Angeles Dodgers—is married to Mia Hamm, an international women's soccer star.

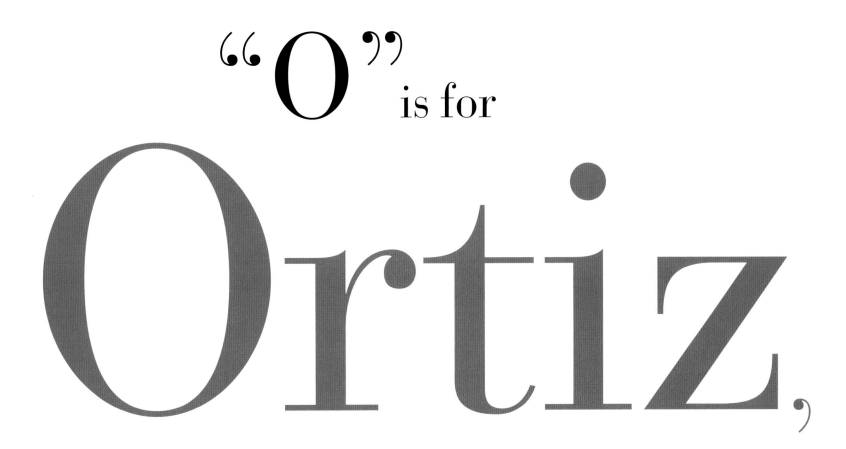

# "O" is for Ortiz,

Whose hits fueled the streak
That sent the Yanks reeling
And helped climb the peak.

**David "Big Papi" Ortiz came aboard in 2003 and quickly established himself as a force** in the middle of the Sox lineup. The genial giant's slugging led the epic comeback against the Yankees in the 2004 ALCS that made possible the team's World Series crown that year. He kept up that pace in the seasons that followed, never falling below the 30-homer, 100-RBI mark in any of his five Red Sox campaigns through the 2007 championship year.

# "P" is for Pesky,

Whose throw came too late.
Some people still ask, "Did he hesitate?"

**Johnny Pesky was the shortstop on the pennant-winning Red Sox team of 1946**. He had an excellent major league career, but is famous mostly for the play on which the St. Louis Cardinals' Enos Slaughter scored from first base on a single to give his team the winning run in the seventh and deciding game of that year's World Series. Pesky took the relay from outfielder Leon Culberson and may have hesitated an instant before throwing the ball to home. Pesky said he didn't delay, but others said he did. Whatever the case may be, most observers agreed that the throw wouldn't have arrived in time to catch the sliding Slaughter.

# "Q" is for the question:

# Why Lord, why oh why, did Bill Buckner Let that ground ball get by?

**A blunder even more famous than Pesky's took place in the sixth game of the 1986 World Series,** which pitted the Red Sox against the New York Mets. Boston led the Series three games to two and was ahead 5–3 going into the bottom of the tenth inning at Shea Stadium, but after the first two New York hitters were retired, the Mets scored a run on three singles and another on a wild pitch. Then, with a runner on second base, Mookie Wilson hit a bouncer through the legs of BILL BUCKNER, the Boston first baseman, and the winning run scored. The Mets went on to win the seventh game and the Series. Like Pesky, Buckner was an outstanding player, but is remembered mostly as a World Series "goat."

# "R" is for Ramirez,

A hip-hop baseballer,
But with runners on base
No player stands taller.

**With his baggy uniform and many-braided hair Manny Ramirez** makes a lackadaisical appearance, but he's all business with a bat in his hands. Over 15 Major League seasons through 2007, the last seven with the Red Sox, the native of the Dominican Republic hit 490 home runs and drove in 1,604 runs while making the American League All-Star team every year from 1998 through 2007. Despite having missed many regular-season games with injuries in 2007, Ramirez excelled in the playoffs. His four homers in those games hiked his career postseason total to a record 24.

# "S" is for Schilling.

Whose stocking dripped red,
But he battled the Red Birds
And left them for dead.

**Curt Schilling is another "big game" pitcher whose most dramatic wins came with the 2004 Red Sox.** That year he won Game 6 of the League Championship Series and Game 2 of the World Series despite a right-ankle tendon injury that required stitches to stabilize. The incision leaked but he still won Game 6 of the ACLS and Game 2 of the World Series. The bloody sock he wore while throwing six strong innings of the latter game was sent to the Baseball Hall of Fame. He came through again for the Sox in the 2007 playoffs after an injury-plagued regular season.

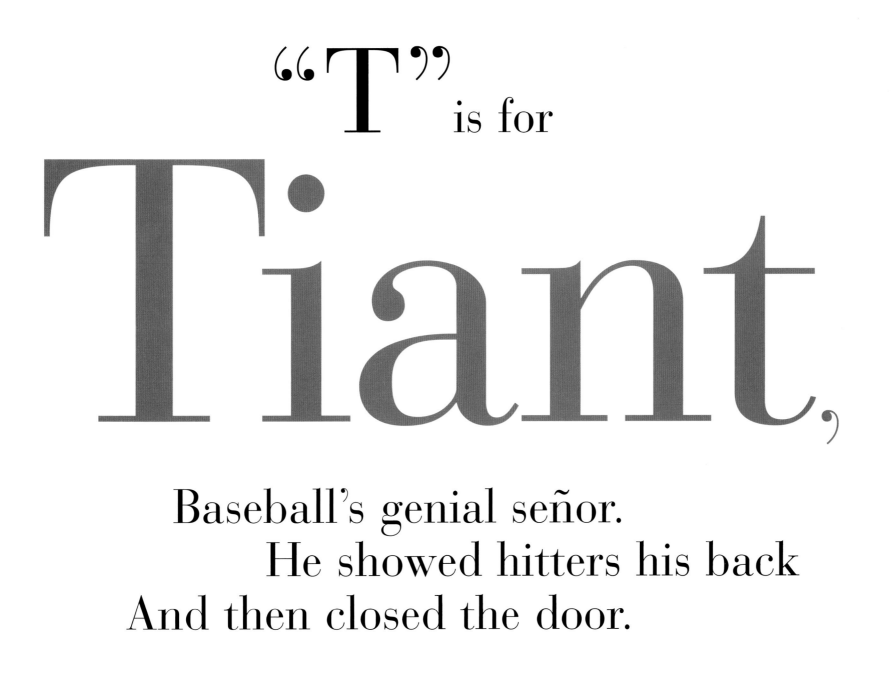

# "T" is for Tiant,

Baseball's genial señor.
He showed hitters his back
And then closed the door.

**Luis Tiant, who was born in Cuba, dazzled major league hitters** with his twisting deliveries for 19 seasons, eight of which (1971–1978) were spent with the Red Sox. He had some of his best years in Boston, posting 122 of his 229 career victories there and winning 20 or more games in three different seasons (1973, 1974, and 1976). He was a popular player whose trademark was a postvictory cigar—Cuban, of course.

# "U" is for Umpire,

Who, though fans may howl
Still have the last word:
Safe or out, fair or foul.

# "V" is for Varitek,

A captain courageous.
The skills he possesses
Are downright outrageous.

**Jason Varitek has spent his entire major league career in Boston**, establishing himself as the Red Sox's starting catcher in 1999 and holding that position through the 2007 championship year. Big, rugged, and durable, he's a solid hitter and an accomplished receiver, as well as a leader on and off the field. That last quality was recognized in 2005 when he became only the third Sox player to be named team captain, following Carl Yastrzemski (1969–1983) and Jim Rice (1986–1989).

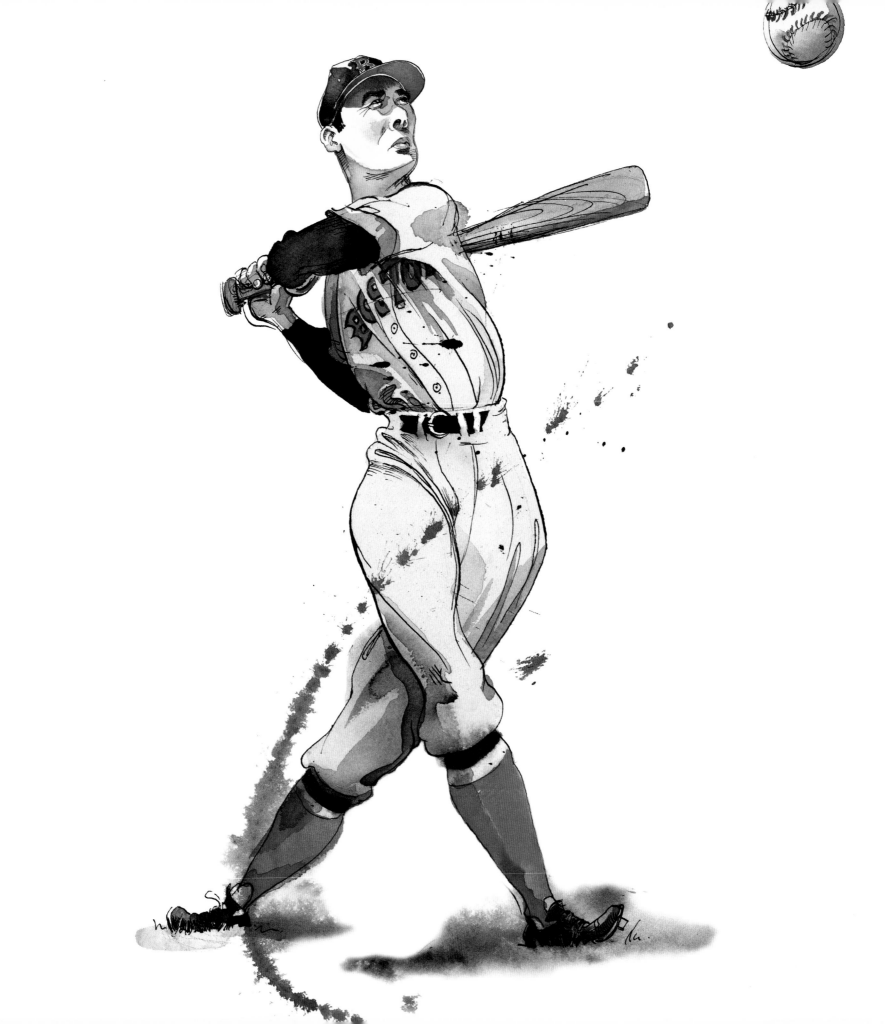

#  "W" is for Williams,

Whose picture-perfect swing
Made Fenway fans cheer
When his home runs took wing.

**Ted Williams was the greatest hitter in Red Sox history**, and perhaps in all of baseball's as well. Combining superb physical coordination with an analytical approach to the batter's art, the "Splendid Splinter" had a career average of .344, 2,654 hits, and 521 home runs over 19 seasons ending in 1960—figures that would have been considerably higher had he not missed all or most of five seasons for military service in World War II and the Korean War. His .406 batting average in 1941 was the last time a major leaguer hit .400 or better for a full campaign. In his last turn at bat, at Fenway Park on September 26, 1960, he hit a home run.

# "X" is for "Double X"

The great Jimmie Foxx.
Some of his best work
Was with the Red Sox.

**Jimmie Foxx succeeded Babe Ruth as baseball's premier power hitter, bashing 534 home runs** in a career that spanned 21 years (1925–1945). Seven of those seasons (1936–1942) were with the Red Sox, including the 1938 campaign in which he hit 50 home runs and drove in 175. Foxx not only hit lots of homers, he also hit them hard and far. One of his blows shattered a seat in the distant reaches of Yankee Stadium.

# "Y" is for Denton "Cy" Young,

Whose win total is why
The awards for best pitcher
Are nicknamed "the Cy."

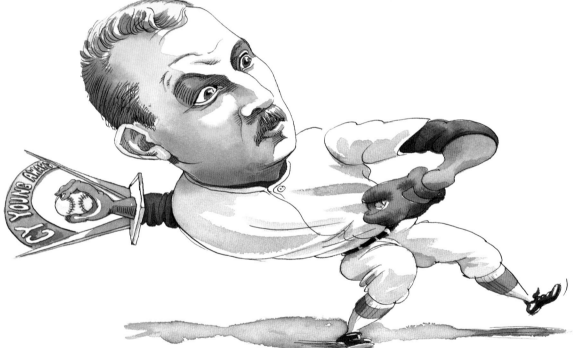

**"Cy" (for "Cyclone") Young was baseball's all-time winningest pitcher**; his career victory count of 511 isn't likely to be broken. A large, sturdy man, the right-hander played at a time (1890–1911) when starting pitchers commonly threw 40 or more complete games in a season, but he stood out even in that iron-man era. In his eight seasons with the Red Sox (1901–1908), he won 20 or more games six times, and his win total in Boston (192) was a team record that he later shared with Roger Clemens. Baseball's annual awards for the best pitcher in each league are named for him.

# "Z" is for

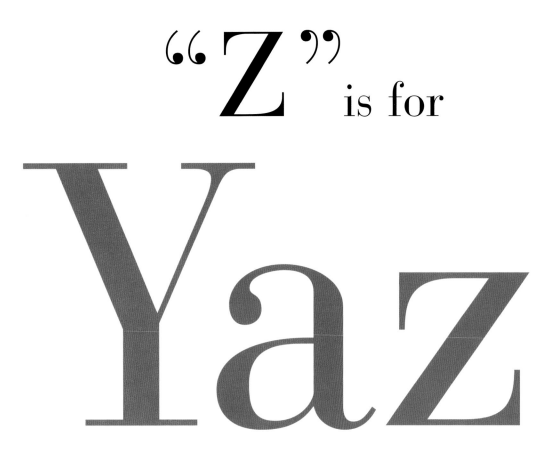

## Yaz

That's Carl Yastrzemski.
For 23 seasons
His name topped the marquee.

**Carl "Yaz" Yastrzemski started out as a shortstop, but changed to the outfield** upon joining the Red Sox and, over 23 seasons (1961–1983), became a fixture in front of Fenway Park's famous left-field wall. Yaz played in a record 3,308 games in a Boston uniform and tops the team's all-time list in seven batting categories. In 1967 he became the last player to win baseball's Triple Crown, leading the American League in hitting (.326), home runs (44), and runs batted in (121).

*Purchase high quality 18x24 archival prints and*
*other products of your favorite Red Sox at:*

Library of Congress Control Number for first edition: 2004107493

This book is available in quantity at special discounts for your group or organization.
For further information, contact:
    Triumph Books
    542 South Dearborn Street
    Suite 750
    Chicago, Illinois 60605
    312. 939. 3330
    Fax 312. 663. 3557

Printed in China
ISBN 978-1-60078-087-5